Garrick's vagary: or, England run mad. With particulars of the Stratford Jubilee.

Gale ECCO Print Editions

Relive history with *Eighteenth Century Collections Online*, now available in print for the independent historian and collector. This series includes the most significant English-language and foreign-language works printed in Great Britain during the eighteenth century, and is organized in seven different subject areas including literature and language; medicine, science, and technology; and religion and philosophy. The collection also includes thousands of important works from the Americas.

The eighteenth century has been called "The Age of Enlightenment." It was a period of rapid advance in print culture and publishing, in world exploration, and in the rapid growth of science and technology – all of which had a profound impact on the political and cultural landscape. At the end of the century the American Revolution, French Revolution and Industrial Revolution, perhaps three of the most significant events in modern history, set in motion developments that eventually dominated world political, economic, and social life.

In a groundbreaking effort, Gale initiated a revolution of its own: digitization of epic proportions to preserve these invaluable works in the largest online archive of its kind. Contributions from major world libraries constitute over 175,000 original printed works. Scanned images of the actual pages, rather than transcriptions, recreate the works *as they first appeared.*

Now for the first time, these high-quality digital scans of original works are available via print-on-demand, making them readily accessible to libraries, students, independent scholars, and readers of all ages.

For our initial release we have created seven robust collections to form one the world's most comprehensive catalogs of 18th century works.

Initial Gale ECCO Print Editions collections include:

History and Geography
Rich in titles on English life and social history, this collection spans the world as it was known to eighteenth-century historians and explorers. Titles include a wealth of travel accounts and diaries, histories of nations from throughout the world, and maps and charts of a world that was still being discovered. Students of the War of American Independence will find fascinating accounts from the British side of conflict.

Social Science

Delve into what it was like to live during the eighteenth century by reading the first-hand accounts of everyday people, including city dwellers and farmers, businessmen and bankers, artisans and merchants, artists and their patrons, politicians and their constituents. Original texts make the American, French, and Industrial revolutions vividly contemporary.

Medicine, Science and Technology

Medical theory and practice of the 1700s developed rapidly, as is evidenced by the extensive collection, which includes descriptions of diseases, their conditions, and treatments. Books on science and technology, agriculture, military technology, natural philosophy, even cookbooks, are all contained here.

Literature and Language

Western literary study flows out of eighteenth-century works by Alexander Pope, Daniel Defoe, Henry Fielding, Frances Burney, Denis Diderot, Johann Gottfried Herder, Johann Wolfgang von Goethe, and others. Experience the birth of the modern novel, or compare the development of language using dictionaries and grammar discourses.

Religion and Philosophy

The Age of Enlightenment profoundly enriched religious and philosophical understanding and continues to influence present-day thinking. Works collected here include masterpieces by David Hume, Immanuel Kant, and Jean-Jacques Rousseau, as well as religious sermons and moral debates on the issues of the day, such as the slave trade. The Age of Reason saw conflict between Protestantism and Catholicism transformed into one between faith and logic -- a debate that continues in the twenty-first century.

Law and Reference

This collection reveals the history of English common law and Empire law in a vastly changing world of British expansion. Dominating the legal field is the *Commentaries of the Law of England* by Sir William Blackstone, which first appeared in 1765. Reference works such as almanacs and catalogues continue to educate us by revealing the day-to-day workings of society.

Fine Arts

The eighteenth-century fascination with Greek and Roman antiquity followed the systematic excavation of the ruins at Pompeii and Herculaneum in southern Italy; and after 1750 a neoclassical style dominated all artistic fields. The titles here trace developments in mostly English-language works on painting, sculpture, architecture, music, theater, and other disciplines. Instructional works on musical instruments, catalogs of art objects, comic operas, and more are also included.

The BiblioLife Network

This project was made possible in part by the BiblioLife Network (BLN), a project aimed at addressing some of the huge challenges facing book preservationists around the world. The BLN includes libraries, library networks, archives, subject matter experts, online communities and library service providers. We believe every book ever published should be available as a high-quality print reproduction; printed on-demand anywhere in the world. This insures the ongoing accessibility of the content and helps generate sustainable revenue for the libraries and organizations that work to preserve these important materials.

The following book is in the "public domain" and represents an authentic reproduction of the text as printed by the original publisher. While we have attempted to accurately maintain the integrity of the original work, there are sometimes problems with the original work or the micro-film from which the books were digitized. This can result in minor errors in reproduction. Possible imperfections include missing and blurred pages, poor pictures, markings and other reproduction issues beyond our control. Because this work is culturally important, we have made it available as part of our commitment to protecting, preserving, and promoting the world's literature.

GUIDE TO FOLD-OUTS MAPS and OVERSIZED IMAGES

The book you are reading was digitized from microfilm captured over the past thirty to forty years. Years after the creation of the original microfilm, the book was converted to digital files and made available in an online database.

In an online database, page images do not need to conform to the size restrictions found in a printed book. When converting these images back into a printed bound book, the page sizes are standardized in ways that maintain the detail of the original. For large images, such as fold-out maps, the original page image is split into two or more pages

Guidelines used to determine how to split the page image follows:

• Some images are split vertically; large images require vertical and horizontal splits.
• For horizontal splits, the content is split left to right.
• For vertical splits, the content is split from top to bottom.
• For both vertical and horizontal splits, the image is processed from top left to bottom right.

GARRICK's VAGARY:

OR,

ENGLAND RUN MAD.

With PARTICULARS of the

STRATFORD JUBILEE.

Furor O Socii, quæ tanta Infania Cives !   VIRG.

What epidemic Madnefs thro' the Land !

LONDON:

Printed for S Bladon, No 28, in Paternofter-Row, 1769.

PREFACE.

THE immediate Object of this Performance being the conftituent Members of our World dramatic, Male and Female, with their manifold Appendages; it is fitting in order to give the Piece a more kindred Complexion to them, than Pamphlets in general have, to caft it into fomewhat of a theatrical Form, tho' but in a defultory Series of irregular Scenes, wherein no ftrict Regard fhall be paid to either the Ariftotelian or Horatian Rules of Art, commanding a fcrupulous Adherence to the three Unities of Place or Scene, of Time, and of Action, Injunctions to which our Shakefpeare but feldom, if ever, attended.

The Effect now propofed is, by fuch a mifcellaneous Production, to prefent to the Public a laughable What d'ye call it, fome Thing or other, preceded by a Prologue, and followed by an Epilogue.

But perhaps an acute-nofed Critic, *homo nafutule*, might fmell out here, as hath often been the Cafe in the Works of many an Author,

As learn'd Commentators view
In Homer more than Homer knew,

That

That altho' unconfcioufly as well as uninten tionally to myfelf, I have hit upon the three Unities, and thus elaboiately attempt to maintain that Doctrine.

1ft, The Unity of Scene is undeniable in Regard to thofe who go from London to Stratford, and return from Stratford to London by the fame Road, ftaging at the fame Inns, becaufe the moft abandoned Caviller cannot have the Effrontery to infinuate even the Poffibility of any Variation in the Article of Diftance, as its being longer or fhorter either Way—

2d, Unity of Time conveyeth to all literary Minds an Idea of fome particular Period, to which the Adjective *one* can be added, as one Hour, one Day, one Week, one Month, one Year No Work of poetical Invention is allowed to extend farther, and that is the indifputable Prerogative of the Imperial Epic Mufe, as vouched for by Virgil's Æneid.

The Preparations, Progreffions, and final Execution of the Stratford Jubilee, having been commenced in London, thence carried along the Road thither, thro' feveral Counties, for their Exhibition there, and then, afterwards, the bringing their Remains up, as well as the People who went down, could require a no lefs Duration of Time than from Sunday to Sunday inclufive, one Week; there is *Unity* of Time manifeftly eftablifhed.

3d, The

3d, The laft Unity is that of Action. Here Hypercriticifm afks, with a triumphal Leer, "What Denomination deferves the Bufinefs from London to Stratford, as well as thence back again," and through a wanton Impatience thus pertly anfwers to its own Queftion; "the Bufinefs or Action was one continued Series of Folly."

A Doubt having arifen in our impartial Bofom as to the Validity of fuch Proofs, we fufpend either giving, or refufing our own, or entreating the Public's Rejection of, or implicit Affent to them, till in Confequence of a calm and difpaffionate reading or hearing of the following Allegations now to be paffed in Review.

P R O-

—

PROLOGUE.

To be Spoken, or Sung

O For the Genius of laughing Dean *Swift*,
  For who could a Joke set better adrift?

Grant me, kind *Momus*, with Humour to tell,

What Scenes at *Stratford on Avon* befell

O vary my Style as the Subject flows,

Now ambling in Rhime, now trotting in Profe;

True to my Motto, till hoarse did I baul,

What Devil from Hell poffeffes ye all?

GARRICK'S VAGARY:

OR,

ENGLAND RUN MAD.

SCENE I.

The BEDFORD COFFEE-HOUSE.

Enter Nettle, Fanciful, *and* Lurcher, *three critical Play-house Frequenters, the first angry, the others laughing.*

Nettle.

DO now be quiet—Pray let me get into yon Corner, that my Ears may have a soothing Recess from the perpetual and grating Din with which they

are

are now moſt cruelly perſecuted.——
Whitherſoever —I go, I can hear of nothing but Stratford, Avon, Shakeſpeare, Jubilee, and I know not what!

Fanciful.

What it means, I ſuppoſe ——

Lurcher.

You ſuppoſe! You do not mean to
affront the Gentleman, I hope, by
this indirect Implication of a Doubt
concerning his Knowledge of Men and
Books.

Nettle.

Why, really Gentlemen, I do not
know well what to think of both, or
either of you——whether you mean to
be ſerious or jocoſe with your humble
Servant; tho', by the collected Steadi-
neſs of your Features, Mr. Lurcher, I
ſhould

should incline to think the former, yet, by a seemingly covered Archness in your Expression, I have some Inkling to surmise the latter——Be that as it may, I care not; but be assured, you, Sir, as well as your Friend, Mr. Fanciful, whom I know to be of a smiling Disposition, that I understand thoroughly the Purport, the Tenour, the Meaning, the Drift, and utmost Significancy of the Word Jubilee : and, from that consummate Knowledge arises my present Indignation against the People of England, Men, Women, and Children, Clergymen, Soldiers, Lawyers, Physicians, such as have no Patients, those who have chuse not to quit them, by Reason of the golden Rule—-to see them, I say, running out of Town, pell-mell, after a Brat of *Judaism*, a since foster-Child of *Popery*, now, forsooth, revived by an Actor, to the very imminent and

B 2 most

moſt alarming Danger both of Church
and State——As a good Engliſhman, and
a true Proteſtant, I feel much Concern,
am patriotically hurt, at ſuch unwarrant-
able doings, at ſo papiſtical a Manœuvre,
at this Time too.——I wonder how our
Biſhops can remain quiet on ſo critical
an Innovation——Let them look to it
in Time, they have more to fear from
its Conſequences than I——

Lurcher.

Why, Sir, you need not wonder at
their Indolence or Supineneſs on this
Occaſion, if you reflect how paſſively
polite, and miniſterially complaiſant they
deported themſelves at the paſſing of the
Jew-Bill——Their ſpecific Philanthropy,
univerſal Benevolence, and profeſſional
Charity for their Fellow Creatures, never
appeared in a more conſpicuous Manner,
than in that delicately trying Circum-
ſtance

ftance which afforded ample Matter of Admiration throughout the Realm.

Fanciful.

Surely you don't think you can take us in, that Way, my dear Lurcher; I know you well , this is one of your fly Jokes, and might pafs on others, not on me——But to be ferious a little, I declare for my own Part, that there never appeared to my Judgment but one Reafon fufficiently cogent to oppofe the Jew-Bill's being carried into Execution.

Nettle.

What Reafon is that, pray ?

Lurcher.

Aye, tell us, for I fhall be glad to know it.

Fan-

Fanciful.

Well, Gentlemen, to satisfy at once your Impatience and Curiosity, that, which may feem to you extraordinary, that Reafon of mine confifts in, and is founded upon an antient Prophecy, declaring, that whenever the Jews fhall have a Kingdom of their own, (which muft inevitably have been the Event in England, had the Act in their Favour taken Place) from the faid fatal Epoch the World is to laft but three Years.

Lurcher.

O! I thank you for this very obliging Information——

Nettle.

Such a Reafon indeed may be adopted in the gay Circles which Mr Fanciful frequents, but can never hope to pafs

cur-

current among ferious Enquirers, or Perfons of ftrong Intellects, and athletic Cogitation——But let us return from trifling, to what we have digreffed from, the Word Jubilee, of whofe Origin, Intendment, &c. I propofe giving you a fuccinct, yet fatisfactory Account. Then you, Mr. Lurcher, in a ferious Way, and you, Mr. Fanciful, in a jocular one, may comment on what I fhall unfold to you; that by fuch a Procefs we may be enabled juftly to afcertain with what Propriety this Term is now forced, or rather perverted, to notify and mifdecorate a new Species of Bacchanalian Revelling at **Stratford** upon Avon.

Fanciful.

Sir, my Ears are all Attention.

Lurcher.

─Lurcher.

And fo are mine──As you advance,
we fhall make our Obfervations.

Nettle.

You are to know, Gentlemen, that
it became cuftomary among the Jews to
fignify, by the Word Jubilee, the Return of every fifth Year, as that following the feven Weeks of Years, at which
wifhed for Period of Time all Bondf-
men were fet free; all Debts were then
abolifhed; all Lands, that had undergone Seizure, or been otherwife aliena-
ted from, reverted, to their original Pro-
prietors──The cultivating of Land was
prohibited during that Year, in which
the Poor claimed all the Fruits of the
Earth as their Right. None but indi-
gent Ifraelites were entitled to this Privilege.

Lurcher.

Lurcher.

There is no Affinity derivable from any of these Articles to the Stratford Affair.

Fanciful.

None in the least——I shall be glad to know if any can be deduced from an etymological Investigation of the Word——

Nettle.

As little, I assure ye; but attend—— " According to many learned Antiquarians, and *Masius* in particular, this Term derives its Origin from the Name of the Inventor of musical Instruments, *Jubal,* whence the Words *Jobel* and *jubilee,* expressed the Year of *Deliverance* and *Remission* ; because it was proclaimed to all by the sounding Heraldry of one of those Instruments. This desirable Proclamation, on its being

C

first

firſt inſtituted, and long after, was made known by the Sound of a not more ele-vated Conveyancer than that of a *Ram's Horn.*——

Lurcher.

Here, indeed, Mr. Garrick, and his Brother Managers, may introduce a not quite inapplicable Similarity, and by which they would greatly oblige the Public, at leaſt the taſteful Part of it; and that is, by their procuring the Stage's *Deliverance* from the many undramatic Beaſts of Lumber under which it now groans. That Deed would certainly effec-tuate for them an entire *Remiſſion* of all critically candid Reſentment on this very provoking Account.

Fanciful.

Well hit off, I ſwear; but pray don't forget propoſing to jubilee the De-linquents

linquents out of Town, after their Dif-
miffion, with a well founded Chorus of
Ram's Horns.

Nettle.

Naturam expellas furcâ licet ufque recurret
HOR.

I fee it were a vain Hope to expect
a Reformation in you, Gentlemen ; becaufe you [*to Lurcher.*] will never let
flip an Opportunity of being farcaftical ;
nor you [*to Fanciful.*] of playing the
Wag——I cannot help confeffing, that
even from my Gravity you had almoft
extorted a Laugh. But ftop your Mer-
riment, that I may continue my Narrative.
" In Imitation of the Jews, the Chrif-
tians have adopted the Name, and in-
ftituted *Jubilees*, which commenced under the Papacy of Boniface VIII. in the
Year 1300, and are now practifed every

twenty-

twenty-five Years , but thefe relate only to the *Forgivenefs of Sins*, and the *Indulgences granted by the Church of Rome,* with the additional Privilege of exhibiting a thoufand Pranks, Follies, and pious Buffooneries in Mafquerade.

Lurcher.

As for the *Forgivenefs of Sins*, few of our theatrical Folks, I believe, think at all about it, from an internal Conviction, perhaps, that it would be to little or no Purpofe——and they trouble their Heads too as little about the *Indulgences* of Rome, in that Article, at leaft, good Proteftants; while they are fupported by the much more defirable *Indulgence* of humane Britifh Audiences,

Fanciful.

There I join with you, Friend Lurcher, and am highly pleafed to find fo pat an
Apo-

Apology from the Pope of Rome for the Pope of Drury-Lane's introducing a Mafquerade, as one of the neceffary Ingredients for completing a Jubilee.

Nettle.

What! at your fevere and fly Jokes again?——You'll not let me finifh at this Rate——Pray interrupt me no more, and I fhall foon have done——

Lurcher.

Well, we will animadvert no more till you fhall have concluded.

Fanciful.

Agreed.

Nettle.

I rely on your joint Promife——" In the following Manner is the Jubilee opened at Rome——The Pope proceeds from St.

St. Peter's Church to open the Holy-
Gate, which at other Times is walled
up, and never opened but on the Occa-
sion of this grand Ceremony. His
mitred Supremacy holdeth in his Hand
a *golden Hammer*, with which he knocks
three Times at the Gate, and repeats
these Words *Aperite mihi Portas Justi-
tiæ*, &c. " Open the Gates of Righte-
ousness unto me, I will go in thro' them,
and praise the Lord." Whereupon the
Masons go to work, and demolish the
Wall with which the Gate had been stopt
up---That Operation over, his Holiness
kneels down before it, and the Penitentiaries sprinkle him with holy Water.

That Part of the Ceremony being
over, the Pope takes up the Cross, begins
to sing the *Te Deum*, and penetrates into the Church, followed by all the Eccle-
siastics——Three Cardinal Legates are,
in the mean Time, sent to open the
three

three other Holy Gates that are in the several Churches of St. Paul, St. Mary the greater, and St. John Lateran.

At the Expiration of the Holy, or the Jubilee Year, the established Usage of shutting up those Holy Gates is as follows. The Pope begins by *blessing the Stones and the Mortar*, then lays the first Stone, and leaves there *twelve Boxes of Gold, and Silver Medals; after which the Holy Gates are walled up as before, and continues so till the next Jubilee——"*, I have now, Gentlemen, fulfilled my Promise, so you are free to set about descanting thereon as fast as you chuse, nor shall I be displeased to hear your whimsical Conjectures, so you do not strain the Matter too far.

Fanciful.

Omnis Comparatio clandicat: Every Comparison limps, was a very wise Ob-
serva-

fervation made by an antient Latin
Writer; and that Truth will appear moft
glaringly, in my attempt to make an
illuftrative Application here——Firft,
" As the Pope goes to St. Peter's Church
to open, &c." So did our Rofcius go to
that of Stratford to have opened its
Holy Gates, and for this Occafion *only*
——To vindicate a Parity in Regard to
what follows, we muft fubftitute one of
the Spectators drawn thither by Curio‑
fity, and prefenting himfelf at the great
Door of the Booth, then the Allufion
will flide on glibly——and, *holding a
golden Hammer in his Hand*, that is, the
Ticket, which coft him a Guinea, *he
knocks at the Gate three Times*, from a
natural Impatience to get in, and have
a good Seat, *repeating thefe Words, Aperite mihi Portes juftitiæ*, &c. Open the
Door, for I have a juft Right to go in
and hear the Praife of Shakefpeare. *The
Mafons*

Mafons fall to work, and break down, &c.
which is *tantamount o* ; "the Perfons appointed to receive the Tickets open the
Door, and let him in---*which done, the Pope
kneels down, and the Penitentiaries befprin-
kle him with holy Water*---fo the Spec-
tator being entered, fits down, (being a
much eafier Situation than kneeling)
and all thofe of his Acquaintance, now
become repentant for the Expences at-
tendant on this Solemnity, pay him their
Compliments from every Side ; becaufe,
by the French Words *l'Eau benite de la
Cour*, i. e. the holy Water of the
Court, nothing more is meant than
fine Words, and parading Declarations,
without any Intent of fulfilling them.

D   *Lurcher,*

Lurcher.

By Jupiter, that is well hit off—I thank you---I envy you for it---Previous to that brilliant Difcovery, you had hobbled on but in a very aukward Manner, which made me to look on you fometimes with an Eye of Compaffion.

Nettle.

I profefs too, Mr. Lurcher, I am not a little exhilarated by the ingenious Feftivity of that Conceit---It denotes, moreover, the Gentleman's having had a French Education, and his knowing that Language well---Proceed then, Mr. Fanciful---

Fanciful.

Fanciful.

No, Gentlemen, I know my Intereſt too well: and, ſince you are both now in ſo favourable an Opinion of me, I will not run the riſk of loſing it ; therefore do you, good Maſter Lurcher, take up the Subjeƈt where I left off.

Lurcher.

With all my Heart---but let me think a few Moments---*Then taking up the Croſs,* &c.---Here we are to ſubſtitute our *Roſcius,* entering the Booth at *Stratford,* followed by all his theatrical Tribe, of various Denominations ; *and then, taking up* not *the Croſs,* but the *Ode,* he begins to read, ſoon after his vocal Auxiliaries to ſing ; ſo on alternately to the End. *In the mean Time, three Car-*

dinal-

dinal-Legates to have three other holy Gates opened, &c.--- like unto this Act of Courtefy, three Actors, dreffed for Shakefpeare's three Cardinals, Wolfey, Campejus, and Pandolph, might be fent to the three different Departments of the Booth, 1*mo*, That in the Front, 2*do*, That on the Right, and 3*tio*, That on the left Hand, to fee that fo refpectable a Company was duly accommodated---*When the holy Year is expired*, the holy Gates are *fhut up*---fo, the Stratford Jubilee over, the Door of the Booth is to allow no more Admiffion of Perfons, and for the very good Reafon that it will, in all Probability, be pulled down, and carried away---The Pope, after *he has bleft the Mortar and Stones*, lays *the firft Stone*---fo Mr. Garrick might give a very effectual Bleffing for Mortar, as well as Stones, and lay the firft himfelf, towards erect-

ing

ing an Obelifk commemorative of the Ground whereon the Booth ftood, and there to continue till the next Jubilee ---The Pope leaves behind him *twelve Boxes of Gold and Silver Medals.* How far Rofcius *might chufe to imitate* this Example *I cannot pretend* to fay.

Fanciful.

But this I am fure of, that befides his own expending on this Occafion, which borders even on royal Munificence, he is the Caufe of a very confiderable Sum of Money being circulated at Stratford, and all around, for which the Inhabitants there muft ever retain a grateful Remembrance.

Nettle.

There is one Thing fticks with me yet. What Neceffity was there for an Oratorio?

Fanciful.

Fanciful.

Becaufe, I fuppofe, no other kind of Performance would be allowed of in the Church.

Lurcher.

Well then, if abfolutely neceffary, why was a Choice made of *Judith?*

Nettle.

Aye, that is what I fhould be glad to know.

Fanciful.

Why the Reafon is very obvious--- there being no Oratorio called *William* to be done in immediate honour of him- felf, a judicious Approximation was thus made, he having had no Sons, by complimenting him thro' his eldeft Daughter *Judith*---

Nettle.

Nettle.

That is too much, Sir, there is no
hearing any more.

[*Exit.*

Lurcher.

O! my dear Fanciful, that is too
grofs a Hum for me to fwallow---So,
your humble Servant---

[*Exit.*

Fanciful.

I am glad they are gone, being almoft
tired of fpinning out the Subject fo long
——I'll go and amufe myfelf for the
reft of the Evening at the facetious Re-
prefentation of a Character that can
never fatiate, the truly abfurd and favou-
rite *Cadwallader.*

[*Exit.*

SCENE

SCENE II.

A Chamber in an Inn on the Road to Stratford upon Avon, a Table with a Bottle Glasses, &c.

HEMLOCK, CROTCHET.

Hemlock.

CONSIDERING that we rode but common Hacks, and set out rather late from London, I think we we have made tolerable Speed.

Crotchet.

We shall get to Stratford early enough in the Afternoon To-morrow for the Completion of my Plan to defeat this prodigal Novelty of celebrating the Memory

mory of an idle Deer-Stealer—Since
Mafter *Rofcius* had the Petulance to re-
ject my Comedy, I will do for his Vagary, and have already fent him an an-
mous Hint of it in Rhime.

As in *Farquhar*'s Play young *Jubilee Dicky*
    Is repentantly forc'd to cry *peccavi*;
Ev'n fo with our Pens expect we fhall lick you,
    Thou vain and prefumptuous *Jubilee Davy*.

Hemlock.

What vile Trafh! But no Matter,
as we are both embarked in the fame
Bottom. The Fellow does not want
fome fmattering of Senfe, but will, in
the Devil's Name, ftrive againft Nature
to be a Poet.---Upon my Word, that is
a pretty jingling Conceit of yours---
unborrowed, and original, I warrant.

Crotchet.

Certainly.

E   *Hemlock.*

Hemlock.

In return for that pert-jubilee Gentleman's treating a Tragedy of mine in a not more obliging Manner than he did your Comedy, I purpose to fee the Vanity of him and his vagrant Crew adequately punifhed on this Occafion, and made to undergo fome ftinging Mortification.

Crotchet.

I am actuated with a like Inclination of difturbing this ridiculous Pageantry; and if you communicate your Scheme to me, fhall unfold mine to you, that we may mutually affift in forwarding each other's Plan.

Hemlock.

That will I, Sir, and cheerfully---My Project to put a Stop to this riotous and unjuftifiable Meeting, fo hurtful to all the neighbouring Manufactures,

making

making all the Folks run fo mad abroad,
and gad, for what? For a Player's pa-
negyrifing a Player, at a Time too when
the gathering of Crowds gives fo great
Offence to Government, I found upon
legal Authority, as I fhall now read to
you in this Extract from a parliamentary
Act.

" Be it declared and enacted by
the King's moft excellent Majefty, by,
and with the Advice and Confent of
the Lords Spiritual and Temporal and
Commons in this prefent Parliament
affembled, and by the Authority of the
fame, that from, and after the Twenty-
Fourth Day of June, 1736, every Perfon who fhall for Hire, Gain, or Re-
ward, act, reprefent, or perform, or
caufe to be acted, reprefented, or performed, any Interlude, Tragedy, or Comedy, Opera, Play, Farce, or other
Entertainment of the Stage, or any

Part,

Part, or Parts thereof, in Cafe fuch
Perfon fhall not have any legal Settle-
ment in the Town where the fame
fhall be acted, reprefented, or performed, without Authority by Vir-
tue of Letters-Patent from his Majefty,
his Heirs, Succeffors, or Predeceffors,
or without Licence from the Lord Cham-
berlain of his Majefty's Houfhold for
the Time being, fhall be deemed to be
a Rogue and Vagabond, and fhall be
liable and fubject to all Mal-Penalties
and Punifhments, and by fuch Methods
of Conviction, as are inflicted on, or
appointed by the faid Act for the Punifh-
ment of Rogues and Vagabonds, who
fhall be found wandering, begging,
and mifordering themfelves, &c. &c."

Crotchet.

The Spirit of this Act (which is very
ill-digefted, abfurd, nay, an infamous
one,

one, and ought to be repealed for many Reafons, which I have not Leifure now to enforce) apparently makes for you ; but then I doubt that you will be able to procure any Juftices in or about Stratford to carry it into Execution, unlefs there be among them fome kindred and relative Defcendants from the Family that hunted Shakefpeare to London——Befides, methinks there is an evafive Loop-Hole for them to elude any legal Purfuit.

Hemlock.

Which is that, pray ?

Crotchet.

That the Ode to be performed in the Booth has not been acted; therefore does not fall under the penal Denominations recited in your parliamentary Extract.

Hemlock.

Hemlock.

It has been acted at Drury-Lane Theatre privately, to prepare it for a public and money-taking Exhibition at Stratford, and afterwards is to be re-prefented at Drury-Lane Theatre as often as the Public will countenance it—What call you then Proceffion, Mafquerade, &c.? I tell you that every theatrical Man and Woman, that fhall Speak, Sing, Walk, Fiddle, or Dance there, are comprehended in the Act alluded to---There will be fine picking, to have fifty Pounds fterling for every Male and Female Head, though Heaven knows how little is the intrinfic Value moft of them can pretend to!

Crotchet.

I by no Means approve of your Scheme, becaufe it is fraught with too

much

much Danger, and therefore think my own, as the more practicable, to be the more eligible.

Hemlock.

Let me hear it, I am always open to Conviction.

Crotchet.

I mean, by attacking the Pride of the Performers, to raise a Spirit of Mutiny and Revolt amongst them, will hint to them, that this new-fangled Manner of exhibiting the Company with their theatrical Infignia, to ftaring Crowds along the Streets, is a degrading of their Profeffion, and reducing them too nearly on a Level with the formerly defpifed Paraders before the Booths of Bartholomew Fair---for ftrip Bayes of his new-raifed Troops, then what becomes of his imaginary Kingfhip?

Hemlock.

Hemlock.

O you have always loved to be well with the Players——for my part I hate the Wretches, becaufe in general they are as ignorant as Dirt, yet vain as Peacocks. For their infolent Behaviour to me at Times I am refolved to be even with, and make them know the difference between fuch Mifcreants, fuch fecond-hand Exiftences, and me---Damn them, is it not I and other Authors of my Rank that fupply them with daily Bread? Are they not our Parrots? What muft become of them were it not for the words which we put in to their mouths?

Crotchet.

What would alfo become of the Words and Writings of Authors, if there were not fuch Parrots, as you are pleafed to call them, to give Utterance and Energy to their Meaning?---There are,

are, befides, feveral among them whom I efteem as valuable Members in private Life, and admire their Talents in a public Capacity.

Hemlock.

That being the Cafe, Sir, I will travel no longer with you---I fee that I am in Danger of your blowing my Scheme to the Players; and a Perfon who talks fo favourably of muft be bad as any among them. By ——

Crotchet's making no other Reply but with a Laugh, provoked Hemlock's raifing his Voice higher, as well as his Oaths, and almoft to Blafphemy, until a Juftice of the Peace entered fiom a neighbouring Room, to make him preferve Order, pay for the Oaths he had fworn, and obey the Laws.

Hemlock.

I pay you! that would be ftretching Poetical Licence too far indeed——As for the obeying Order, Law, Precept, or

F   Re-

Regulation whatfoever, though laid down by Ariftotle, by Horace, or even thofe of Syntax and Profody, I ever fcorned, as you may fee by my Works [*takes fome out of his Pockets.*] Thefe Memoirs in Profe, two Poems, and three Acts of a Tragedy——match them if you can——I am the Nonfuch of Parnaffus, you Blockhead.

During this Speech, Crotchet contrived to flip out of the Room, paid the Reckoning, ordered his Horfe from the Stable, and returned part of the way back to London that Night, renouncing his idle Intent to interrupt the Stratford Feftivity. Hemlock fwore fo much, and became fo rude 'to the Juftice, that he was obliged to commit him to Prifon, where he remained three Days, until fome Gentlemen of his Acquantance, on their Return from Stratford to London, having got Intelligence of the Tranfaction, procured

his

his Difcharge, and brought him with them to London. The Confinement was, however, fo far lucky as it prevented his being ducked in the Avon; from which poetical River he could not hope to rife a melodious Swan, but, what he hath always been, a cackling, offenfive Goofe.

SCENE III.

STRATFORD UPON AVON.

A Lodging Houfe.

Sir Benjamin Scrutiny, Lord Charles Candid.

Sir Benjamin.

WELL, my dear Lord Charles, I think our Apartment is as pleafantly fituated as poffible in this Town, and from thefe Windows we have a commodious Profpect of all the gaily attiredFiguies as they pafs to and fro.

Lord

Lord Charles.

I could almoſt become poetical on
the Occaſion, and had we not had a
Number of Things to ſee for the ſhort
Time we propoſe being here, I could
find in my Heart to ſit down and write
away, to this rhiming Meaſure, in what
People of Faſhion are pleaſed to call
the eaſy Gentleman-like Stile.

Never a Sight ſo fine was ſeen,
In Stratford Town, or neighb'ring Green,
What rich dreſs'd Ladies, flaunting Beaus,
How fit their ſelves for Raree-ſhews!

Honeſt *Ralph* comes boldly along,
Forcing his Way divides the Throng;
And why ſhou'd he not, ſince he can?
For, Waunds, he's *Shakeſpeare's* Countryman.

Sir Benjamin.

So far, not amiſs, my Lord---

Lord Charles.

O you flatter me, Sir Benjamin---But
what heightens the moving Pictures before us, is the hearty, ſtaring, broad-
faced Earneſtneſs of the ſimple Country-
folks, that form ſuch an entertaining
Con-

Contraſt to the ſpruce, pert, and diſci-
plined Features of the Londoners, laviſh-
ing their Nods, and twinkling with
their Eyes at every Perſon they can pretend the leaſt Knowledge of —

Enter Servant.

My Loid, Notice is given that the
Oratorio is going to begin.

Lord Charles.

An Oratorio! Well---To the Oratorio let us go——

Sir Benjamin.

I attend your Lordſhip.   [*Exit.*

S C E N E IV.

*Lord Charles, Sir Benjamin, on the ſecond
Morning of the Feſtival, as they are going
to the Booth to hear the Ode.*

Sir Benjamin.

WHAT an Original and teſty
Mortal that is, whom we have
got rid off; ever torturing himſelf

to find Fault, and looking out for the worſt Side of Things---he can't forgive Mr. Garrick this very laudable Under-taking---" Why ſhould he, forſooth? and Why? and Why? and Why?" to all his Why's my Anſwer is, and every unbiaſſed Perſons will be, that no other Individual could have been the principal Agent here, with ſo much Propriety. This Project too may be conſidered, in ſome Meaſure, as the diſchaiging a Debt of Gratitude; becauſe to the immortal Bard's Writings, the admirable Performer at his firſt launching on the Stage, in the Characters of Richard, Lear, &c. owed the eſtabliſh-ing of that Fame, which has ſince procured to him an ample Fortune; a Part whereof cannot, ſurely, be better employed than on an Occaſion like this.

Lord Charles.

Really, Sir Benjamin, I think ſuch ridiculous Objections deſerve rather

Con-

Contempt than to be ferioufly refuted---
How many Places contended for Homer's Birth? What Nation, any way
civilized, is not proud of having pro-
duced a Genius, and exults at every
Mark of publick Honour that is paid
to him. For my Part I am not only
pleafed with, but obliged to Mr. Garrick, for his having been chiefly in-
ftrumental in fo commendable, nay fo
patriotic an Inftitution.

Sir Benjamin.

You think very juftly, my Lord---
The Intention in every Thing is to be
attended to; and a generous Mind will
bound over all little Over-fights and un-
forefeen Accidents that may intervene:
fuch as the fall of Rain, we are furprifed
with, that prevents Mr. Angelo's fhew-
ing his Skill in Fire-works, as it entirely
fuperfedes the intended Proceffion.

Lord Charles.

How many aching Hearts in and a-
bout

bout Stratford on that Account——Do you know, Sir Benjamin, who is that well looking Gentleman just gone by with folded Arms and down-cast Eyes, muttering to himself with discontented Accents——now in Italian, *Qual cattivo tempo*, now in French, *Quel mauvais temps*, what bad Weather!

Sir Benjamin.

That is the identical Mr. Angelo I just now mentioned to you, whose Mortification gives me some Concern, because I am informed, that he has taken uncommon Pains to make a most elegant Apparatus of Fireworks.

Lord Charles.

The best Way to comfort would be to tell him, that it is not from mere Chance alone this threatning Impediment and dire Consequences of a Storm are gathering round the Town, but that they are caused by the special Mandate and Agency of superior Beings, which

it

it were in vain for weak Mortals to attempt oppofing—And as Venus fhewed
to Æneas in the laſt fatal Night of
Troy, by removing the Film of Morta-
lity from before his Eyes, that it was
not the Greeks, but combined Deities
that worked its final Overthrow; ſo one
might poetically endeavour alleviating
Mr. Angelo's Anxiety by a Suppoſition
of Great Shakefpeare's Shade being returned from Elyſium, and on the Top
of Stratford-Church to have ſung Strains
to this Purport:

Obey me, ye Fairies,
    Whofe Reign o'er the Air is,
And drive Clouds ſcatter'd together,
Stratford afflict with foul Weather;
    For Shame to my Glory,
    It fhan't live in Story,
That I'm to Gun-powder beholding:
    That were a Demerit
    My Fame fhan't inherit,
So bear to the Steward this ſcolding;
Dull *Comments* and *Fireworks* alike I defpife,
Thro' my own native Blaze I foar'd to the Skies,

G   Go

Go tell my lov'd Roscius I've said with a Frown;
That, proudly, I'll shine by no Light but my own.

—

No sooner was this agreeable Mandate given, than away flew the little Gentry, East, West, North, and South. They let not the least Cloud *escape their Search:* On some of which one Party ride a Cock-horse, others drive larger Ones before, and others drag after them the heaviest; till, by aggregating their manifold Collection, the Atmosphere is curdled into a lowering Aspect, that makes the drooping Swans of Avon, from Time to Time, look up with melancholy Eyes, and the sorrowing Naiads to sigh along the Banks, at the Dread of so unwelcome and so rude a Visitation.

Down falls the Rain, and all warm Hopes of a fiery Exhibition are extinguished. The aerial and watry Engineers scout through all the Streets of Stratford and its Purlieus, to see the Act

of

of punifhing in which they are employed
is effectual, that the illuminating Lamps
have undergone a general Devaftation ;
and to break thofe which, by the Bene-
fit of their Situation, might have efcaped.
Here again, allured by the grotefque
Idea, I cannot refrain from ftumbling
out of Profe into Rhime.

Though this, Sir, to *Angelo* may be bad Luck,
What Sport, O ye Gods, for the Fairies and *Puck!*
Lo wherever the Tempeft chances to fail,
They volley with Nut-fhells, that patter like
    Hail ;
And are as delighted with this frolic Job,
As young School-Boys broke loofe an Orchard
    to rob.

Sir Benjamin.

However fuch droll Imagery might con-
tribute to make People fmile, it would, I
fancy, afford but fmall Satisfaction either
to Mr. Angelo or the Difburfers of the
Expence for the intended Fireworks---
The Company is going very faft into

the

the Booth : Let us quicken our Pace,
my Lord.

—

Lord Charles.

Have with you.   I feel a critical Impatience to hear Mr. Garrick read.

S C E N E V.

*Lord Charles, Sir Benjamin, the Morning
of their Departure from Stratford.*

Lord Charles.

SIR Benjamin, I know that you
have as little Paffion for Horfe-
racing as myfelf; therefore ordered my
Equipage to be got ready for our Departure.   The Mafquerade was brilliant : Several of your Acquaintance
enquired of me if you were indifpofed,
as they did not fee you there.

There

Sir Benjamin.

There are but two Motives, and thofe not virtuous Ones, that can hinder a Mafquerade from being one of the dulleft Places in the World; thofe are gaming and intriguing. Gaming I always abhorred, and of intriguing I was never fond; moreover, my Affections are at prefent entirely devoted to a very amiable Object. Without either of thefe two Attractions, what Pleafure can there be to idly ftalk up and down amongft a Croud of People, that by the diverfified Abfurdity of their Dreffes, appear to be fitter Inhabitants for Moorfields than an Affembly of rational Beings?

Lord Charles.

Will you not allow that dancing, for young People, may be an harmlefs Enticement.

Sir

Sir Benjamin.

Perhaps----That depends, however, upon the Circumstance of whom they dance with, &c.

Lord Charles.

I should not have staid long there; but in Consequence of a Whisper, that Messieurs *Foote* and *Macklin*, characteristically dreſt, as *Shylock* the ſnarling merciless Jew, and the merry good-natured Devil upon two Sticks, were to come and ſtrike out between them a Dialogue, which, conſidering what excellent Actors they are, each in his Way, promiſed the higheſt Entertainment. But our Expectation, ſo highly wound up, was ſoon let down by an Information, that immediately after the Ode, Mr. Macklin having diſcovered that the Chambers in
which

which they had lain the Night before were fituated over the Combuftibles prepared for the Fireworks, alarmed Mr. Foote with the Apprehenfion of *a new Gunpowder Plot* being intended againft them; and that, fhould they be blown up, it would give the Laugh fo ftrong on *Garrick's* Side againft them, that were he to hear of it in the other World he fhould be eternally unhappy---The Remonftrance had its Weight, it feems; for off they went---This Incident, to be fure, was odd, but cannot be imagined through any Defign of Mr. Garrick, whom I would never forgive, notwithftanding the Excellence he difplayed in his Part of the Ode Yefterday, which fhewed him in a new Light, and that *Decies decies que placebit*, the oftener feen will give increafing Pleafure; fhould he, I fay, thus clandeftinely fcheme the Deftruction of thofe two Gentlemen, but

con-

continually call upon him with thefe upbraiding Rhimes,—

What a barb'rous Deed, cruel *Garrick*,
Tho' beft Friend* to the Mufe of Warwick§,
    Was't civil or fair,
    To fquib Friends in Air,
How fuch a Lofs repair!

Sir Benjamin.

If this whimfical Reafon, caufed as I fuppofe it did, a Laugh among the Mafqueraders, I was entertained with one to the full as Original of a Movement, that was made Yefterday by Mr. King, from the Place he got up to fpeak in, and by Sprightly, a Student in the Temple, who, like myfelf having no relifh for Mafquerades, vifited

---

* The beft Friend to a Perfon is the He or She who calls forth, and fhews the other's Merit in the moft advantageous Light.

§ Is a *pars pro toto*, and means Warwick, an allowed Figure in Writing, efpecially Poetry.

me

me in your Abfence. When I afked him what he thought was the Caufe, he replied, It was to ftand by a Lady, give his *Macaroni extempore*, to be held in her Hand, but feen by no body elfe, to put him right, fhould he go wrong.

Lord Charles.

O! I am the Gentleman's very humble Servant for that poignant Enucleation ———.

Sir Benjamin.

He is an odd Mortal, and looks at every Thing in a whimfical Light; he defcribed to me the ridiculous Behaviour of fome Authors come down here to each other, hinting by their mock-confequential Looks, Geftures, and Shrugs, as much as to fay, What has brought that Fellow to Stratford, I wonder; can he afford it? who has paid

H for

for him ? Then he compared them, in his humorous way, to their Sifter-Proftitutes of the other Sex ; as the one by Mind fo the other by the Perfon, and both for the fame irrefiftible motive, to live; and againft which all arguments fail: for Choice is but feldom the cafe, on either Side.---

If the humble Night-walkers of the Strand, yielding to an ambitious Impulfe, take devioufly to the Afcent of Catharine-Street, they are driven back with the Charge of Impudence and Vanity unbecoming fuch low Wretches, by the mid-region Nymphs that are ftationed there, who, likewife, muft keep their due Diftance from the ftill higher-lodged Damfels, of Bridges, of Bow-ftreet, and Covent Garden. What a coxcomical laughable Compofition is human Nature !

Lord Charles.

And truly fo it is, Sir Benjamin---
and I do not know any Department of
it, fo grofsly ridiculous in general, as
that of Authors; for the far greater
Number take their feparate Opinions
of each other, and there is not a good
one Living, nay, that can write Englifh.
Name a new Work to them that has
met with the Publick's univerfal Appro-
bation, for inftance, the *Jubilee Ode*
performed at Stratford, how much
better could they have done it !

Sir Benjamin.

Authors, to meet with more Regard
from others, muft learn to be more
equitable, and behave mutually with
more Refpect to themfelves, as is ex-
perienced by thofe Gentlemen in whom

H 2   Genius

Genius and Literature are under the Guidance of Good-Breeding.

Enter Lord Charles's Valet.

My Lord, your Poft-Chariot is ready.

Lord Charles.

Allons, Sir Benjamin----by the Number of Equipages drawn out and looking the way we intend to go, we fhall have Company enough, wherefore let us take the Start of them, as I make my Exit, from our immortal Poet's native Town, with a conclufive poetical Flourifh, or rather farewel Crack of the Pegafean Whip.

Poftillions are mounted; each fmacks the Thong,
Off Score how they drive! and all the Day long,
For *London* away, for *London*'s the Song.
The rapid Zeal of thofe Phaeton Blades,
Their fwift flying Palfreys finks into Jades:
Then is heard on each Road; Gee-ho, Gee-hup,
For as they droye *Down*, fo now they drive *Up*.

S C E N E VI.

The Apollo *Room, at the* Shakespeare's *Head,* Covent - Garden ; *where are discovered, sitting round a Table, on which is a Representation of the* Mulberry *Tree, a Group of* qualified Connoisseurs, *and the Author of this Pamphlet, their weekly Meeting, called the* Mulberry-Club.

The Author.

HERE, Gentlemen, I conclude my sportive Career, my excursionary Trip from London to Stratford, and from Statford to London, back again to the same Ground from which we departed, and that is so dearly beloved by us all, the Garden by Excellence: with which none other can be compared. Sure this is Method, if ever Method was !

Under the Masks of several fancied
Characters, I have attempted to convey
the different Opinions of different Minds
as well as my own, for and against the
late Jubilee, and incidental Events,
without, it is hoped, any Body's taking
Offence thereat, because none was meant.
However, should there be found a Per-
son, or Persons, so unreasonable, I care
not, conscious of my own Innocence as
to that Point.

The

The EPILOGUE.

To be Spoken, or Sung.

WHATEVER began muſt ſure have an End,

'Gainſt ſuch a Truth there are few will con-

tend,

The Lot of this Pamphlet, Fate of the World,

When into Chaos original hurl'd !

Let us then with *Glee* enjoy't while we can,

Life's but a *Catch* ; who can *laugh* is the *Man :*

Come fill up your Glaſſes, honour my Toaſt,

The *Laurel* to him who prais'd *Shakeſpeare* moſt.

Envy defeated is in a Quandary,

While we Bumpers drink to *Garrick's Vagary :*

Can Homage ſo juſt make *England run mad?*

No ; falſe is the Charge · all Worthies 'twill glad.

Let Critics diſſent, or let them agree,

We'll ſing, and dance round the Mulberry-Tree.

CPSIA information can be obtained at www.ICGtesting.com
Printed in the USA
LVOW051626100112

263229LV00014B/38/P